POCKET WISDOM

ROBERT C. SAVAGE

World Wide

A ministry of the Billy Graham Association

1303 Hennepin Avenue
Minneapolis, Minnesota 55403

This special edition is printed with permission
from the original publisher, Tyndale House
Publishers, Inc., Wheaton, Illinois 60187

First printing, May 1984

Library of Congress Catalog Card Number 83-51246
ISBN 0-8423-4905-7, paper
Copyright © 1984 by Robert C. Savage
Printed in the United States of America

With a resounding
"Praise the Lord"
filling my heart and soul,
I dedicate
POCKET WISDOM
to our "Savage tribe."

To wife Wilda,
the "queen bee";

To our four kids,
born in three different countries;
Steve (USA),
Carol (Colombia),
Jim and Judi (both in Ecuador)

To our nine grandchildren,
born in four nations;
Cyndi (Ecuador),
Sharon and Dan (Nigeria),
Alex and Elaine (Mexico),
Lance, Matthew, Bill and Allison
(USA)

"Sentence sermons" . . . "One-liners" . .
"Arrows" . . . "Quotable quotes" . . . or
whatever you want to call them, they
often have a more effective impact (in
ten to fifteen words) than does a standard
length sermon of thirty minutes.

In various churches I've pastored we
have frequently used them on Sunday
nights. At Radio Station HCJB (Quito,
Ecuador) we included them as features
in both English and Spanish broadcasts.
For our Saturday night telecasts (in
Spanish) we called them, "Flechazos al
Corazon" ("Arrows to the Heart").

Pocket Wisdom is a quiver filled with
777 of these arrows. We hope that, as
preachers and teachers, you will tighten
your bowstrings and wing these arrows to
that most important target—the hearts
of your people.

Robert C. Savage
Christiansted, St. Croix

ABILITY

The greatest ability is dependability.

ACCOMPLISHMENT

The man who removes a mountain begins
by carrying away small stones.
(Chinese Proverb)

ACTIVITY

It's one thing to be *active* in our work
for the Lord—quite another thing to be
effective. (T. J. Bach)

ADVERSITY

The Christian faith was made to flourish
in hostile soil.

You can measure a man by the opposition
it takes to discourage him.

It's easy enough to be pleasant
when everything goes like a song;
But the man worthwhile
is the man who can smile
when everything goes dead wrong.

When life knocks you down to your knees
you are in a perfect position to pray.

Don't be afraid of opposition—a kite
rises against the wind, not with it.

It is easier to cope with out-and-out
enemies than with deceptive friends.

Some people suffer in silence—much
louder than others.

(See: Burdens, Difficulties, Problems,
Temptation, Trials)

ADVICE

Most of us would get along well if we used
the advice we give others.

To profit from good advice requires more
wisdom than to give it. (Churton Collins)

AGE

People are funny! Everyone wants to live a
long time, but no one wants to get old!

Just think—twenty-five years from now,
these will be "the good old days."

A man is always as young as he feels, but
seldom as important.

(See: Middle Age, Old Age)

ALCOHOL

I do not think that I should drink.
For when I drink, I do not think.

Isn't it rather foolish for a man to put into his mouth that which takes away his brains?

Some men—battle to the top;
Others—bottle to the bottom.

(See: Liquor)

AMBITION

The number one ambition of every Christian should be that of making every detail of his life an honor and glory to God. "To God be the glory" should be our theme . . . our motto . . . our purpose . . . our goal!

AMIABILITY

To live above with saints we love,
oh, that will be glory.
To live below with saints we know,
well, that's a different story!

ANGER

Some people think they are big shots because they are always exploding!

Men and pins are useless when they lose their heads.

The anger of a good man lasts an instant; that of a meddler, two hours; that of a base man, a day and a night, and that of a great sinner, until death. (Sanskrit)

Never answer an angry word with an angry word. It's the second one that produces a quarrel. (A. A. Nance)

God permits us to be angry in order to gnash our teeth against the devil—not to set us in array against each other.

Striking while the iron is hot is OK, but don't strike while the head is hot.

The trouble with letting off steam is—it only gets you into more hot water.

Don't give anyone a piece of your mind— you need it all yourself!

Swallowing angry words is much easier than having to eat them!

He who blows his stack adds to the world's pollution.

(See: Temper)

APPRECIATION

Some people make a great fuss over a comet in the sky or a total eclipse, but never notice a sunset.

(See: Gratitude)

ART

Modern paintings are like women: You will never enjoy them if you try to understand them!

ATHEISTS

An atheist approaching the end of life made this confession: "There is one thing that mars all the pleasure of my life. . . . I am afraid the Bible is true. If I could know for certain that death is an eternal sleep, I should be happy. But here is what pierces my soul . . . if the Bible is true then I am lost forever."

A good reply to an atheist is to give him an excellent dinner and then ask if he believes there is a cook.

An atheist cannot find God for the same reason a thief cannot find a policeman.

AUTOMOBILES

Most people are having trouble with their cars. The engine won't start and the payments won't stop.

The wheel was man's greatest invention— until he got behind it!

A driver is safest when the roads are dry . . . but the road is safest when the driver is dry.

It takes thousands of nuts to construct an automobile, but only one nut to scatter it all over the road.

(See: Driving)

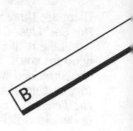

BACKSLIDERS

Backsliding begins when knee-bending stops.

BIBLE

We only really believe as much of the Bible as we practice.

Many Christians mark their Bibles, but their Bibles never mark them!

The Bread of Life never becomes stale.

Study the Bible—to be wise;
Believe the Bible—to be saved;
Practice the Bible—to be holy.

Men do not reject the Bible because it contradicts itself, but because it contradicts *them*.

The Bible is like a lion. It needs no defense. Let it out of its cage, and it will defend itself. (Charles Haddon Spurgeon)

There are three stages of Bible study . . .
The Cod Liver Oil Stage
(you take it like medicine because it is
good for you).
The Shredded Wheat Stage
(dry, but nourishing).
The Peaches and Cream Stage
(a delicious delight).

Show me a man who has a clean,
unspotted Bible, and I will show you a
man with an unclean heart.

But show me a man who has a soiled
Bible, and I will show you a man with a
clean heart. (Basil Malof)

Most people are bothered by passages in
the Bible which they cannot understand.
As for me, the passages in the Bible which
trouble me most are those I *do* understand. (Mark Twain)

The Bible . . .
Know it—in your head;
Stow it—in your heart;
Sow it—in the world;
Show it—in your life!

God cannot open the windows of heaven
for the one who keeps his Bible shut!

A knowledge of the Bible without a college
course is more valuable than a college
course without a knowledge of the Bible.
(William Lyon Phelps)

14

A man has deprived himself of the best there is in all the world, who has deprived himself of this—a knowledge of the Bible. (Woodrow Wilson)

Don't feed on the world's crumbs; get some delicious meals from the Living Bread.

Other books have been written
for our information;
The Bible was given
for our transformation.

A Bible in the hand is worth two on the shelf.

The Bible promises no loaves to the loafer.

BIRTHDAYS
Birthdays are nice to have, but too many of them will kill a person!

BLAME
Many people, when they run into a telephone pole, blame the pole!

BOASTING
The man who has a right to boast doesn't have to.

BORN AGAIN
Born once—you die twice;
Born twice—you die once.

He who is born of God can and should resemble his Father.

BURDENS

A five-year-old girl in the Andean mountain area of South America was carrying her baby brother on her back. A tourist asked her, "Isn't he heavy?" "No," she answered, "he's my brother."

(See: Adversity, Difficulties, Problems, Temptation, Trials)

CALVARY

Calvary is God's blood bank for a sick
world.

CHARACTER

Our strength is shown in the things
we stand for;
Our weakness is shown in the things we
fall for.

Reputation is valuable;
but character is priceless.

Much can be analyzed of a man's character
by noting what excites his laughter.

A good way to keep your feet on the
ground is to put the weight of responsi-
bilities on your shoulders.

Men of genius are admired;
men of wealth are envied;
men of power are feared;
but only men of character are trusted.

What lies *behind* us or *before* us—are tiny matters compared with what lies *in us*.

(See: Conduct, How to Live)

CHASTENING
I'd rather have lots of chastening from the Lord . . . and be usable, than to live a life of ease . . . and be powerless.

CHEERFULNESS
Some people spend all their time scolding sinners, but we must remember people are more attracted to honey than they are to vinegar.

Now is the best time to do something pleasant if you want to have pleasant memories.

A warm smile thaws the icy stare.

You are never fully dressed until you wear a smile.

A loving smile adds a lot to a Christian's face value.

(See: Gratitude, Happiness, Joy, Praise, Smiles, Thankfulness)

CHILDREN
Children, like canoes, are more easily controlled if paddled from the rear.

The way kids turn *out* depends a lot on what time they turn *in*.

When a child is old enough to know that he has sinned, that child is old enough to know that he needs to be saved.
(T. J. Bach)

Isn't it wonderful the way youngsters always brighten up the home? They never turn out the lights!

Let every father and mother realize that when their child is three years of age, they have done more than half they will ever do to mold its character.
(Horace Bushnell)

When a child reaches the age of *accountability,* that child has reached the position of *responsibility.* (T. J. Bach)

Building boys is better than mending men. (I. W. Williamson)

A wayward child is sometimes straightened out by being bent over.

When adults act like children, they are silly. When children act like adults, they are delinquents.

A good formula for raising children—
Give them a pat on the back:
—often enough,
—hard enough,
—low enough.

(See: Parents)

CHRISTIAN

The problem with the average Christian
is that he is just an average Christian.

A true Christian loves not the world,
yet he loves all the world.

It's good to be a Christian and know it.
It's better to be a Christian and *show* it!

Going to church doesn't make you a
Christian any more than going to a garage
makes you an automobile. (Billy Sunday)

CHRISTIANITY

Some have a Christianity that is—
joyless, powerless and juiceless.
    Others have a Christianity that is—
true-blue, snow-white, 100 percent,
crystal-pure, fire-proof, guaranteed and
insured to last forever!

Christianity is like a nail—the more it is
hit, the deeper it goes.

CHRISTMAS

At Christmas, most parents spend more
money on their children than they did
on the honeymoon that started it all.

CHURCH

What kind of a church would my church
be if all of its members were just like me?

Our church is full of willing people; a few are willing to work and the others are willing to let them!

The work of the church is to produce Christian fruit—not religious nuts!

God put the church in the world; Satan seeks to put the world in the church.

At our church we've got everything from soup to nuts, and frankly there is very little soup!

Some churches are certainly sound— sound asleep!

Seven days without church makes one *weak*.

Go to church faithfully. God gives us 168 hours each week—as a minimum give him back at least one of them.

Too many Christians and churches want to settle for a tune-up job when they need a complete overhaul. (Vance Havner)

An ideal church would have members who . . .
Enjoy their faith like the Pentecostals;
Are proud of their church like the Baptists;
Are faithful to the church like the Lutherans;
Finance it like the Christian Reformed;
Are sure of it like the Presbyterians;
Propagate it like the Christian and

Missionary Alliance, and who
Work for it like the Jehovah's Witnesses.

Don't stay away from worship services
because the church is not perfect.

Think how lonesome you would be in a
perfect church.

The church needs less advice on "how to
do it" and more members who are "willing
to do it."

Many church business meetings begin
with the reading of the church covenant,
and end with it being totally ignored.

Going to church in the morning is
nullified if you plan to go to the devil in
the evening.

Some go to church to take a walk,
and others go to laugh and talk.
Some go to church to meet a friend
and some go there an hour to spend.
Some go to church to meet a lover
and some go there a fault to cover.
Some go to learn the preacher's name
and some to criticize his fame.
Some go to church to doze and nod;
and others go to worship God.

The best formula for success in the local
church consists of ten points—
  1. Pray
  2. Work
  3. Pray
  4. Work

5. Pray
6. Work
7. Pray
8. Work
9. Pray
10. Work

Attending church regularly is a wonderful way to get your faith lifted.

CIGARETTES

D. L. Moody was asked: "Are there any verses in the Bible against the use of tobacco?"

He pondered a moment and then said, "No, but I can give you one in favor of it, namely Revelation 22:11—'He which is filthy, let him be filthy still.' "

CIRCUMSTANCES

Circumstances are like a mattress: when we are on top, we rest in comfort; when we are underneath we are smothered.

CIVILIZATION

Our experts, scientists, researchers and politicians have gone to a lot of trouble to improve everything except people.

COMFORT

God does not comfort us to make us comfortable, but to make us comforters. (John Henry Jowett)

God has given me the ministry of comforting the afflicted and afflicting the comfortable. (Vance Havner)

COMMITTEES

Blessed is he who will work as a member of the committee of which he really wanted to be the chairman.

The Ten Commandments are short and to the point, so obviously they were not the work of a committee.

COMMITMENT

Give your life to God; he can do more with it than you can! (Dwight L. Moody)

(See: Consecration, Surrender, Yieldedness)

COMMON SENSE

Common sense is just about the most uncommon thing there is.

COMPLAINING

Don't grumble because you don't have what you want . . . rather be exceedingly grateful you don't get what you deserve!

We mutter and sputter,
we fume and we spurt.
We mumble and grumble,
our feelings get hurt.

We can't understand things,
our vision grows dim.
But all that we need is
surrender to him!

It is not the greatness of my trials but the
littleness of my faith that causes me to
complain.

The wheel that squeaks the loudest gets
the most grease.

(See: Criticism, Faultfinding,
Grouchiness, Grumbling)

CONCEIT

Those who pride themselves on being
hardboiled are often only half-baked.

Give some people an inch and they think
they are rulers.

Conceit is the only disease that makes
everyone sick except the one who has it.

No man can push himself ahead very far
by patting himself on the back.

The fellow who sings his own praise often
gets it in a key that's too high.

He who stands high in his own estimation
is a long way from the top.

The man who has a good opinion of
himself is usually a poor judge of human
nature.

The fellow with an inflated opinion of himself is generally a "flat tire."

(See: Me-first, Pride, Self)

CONDUCT

Be an "amen" Christian, but don't shout it louder than you live it.

If your *walk* is not consistent with your *talk*, you will frequently put your *foot* in your *mouth*.

Be like a good watch—have an open face, busy hands, full of good works, pure gold, and well regulated.

No man has a right to do as he pleases unless he pleases to do right.

Others may doubt what you say, but they will believe what you do.

A good prayer: "O Lord, make me intensely spiritual and at the same time make me thoroughly practical."

It's not enough just to be good—be good for something!

What you do speaks so loudly I can't hear what you say.

When alone—guard your thoughts.
When at home—guard your temper.
When with friends—guard your tongue.

I have resolved never to do anything that I would be afraid to do if it were the last hour of my life. (Jonathan Edwards)

I do not mind how high anyone jumps for joy because of blessings received, if he only walks straight and speaks the truth in love after having touched the ground.

(See: Character, How to Live)

CONFESSION

The easiest thing to confess is—my neighbor's sin.

Oftentimes the man who most desperately needs help is unwilling to admit he has a need.

CONFIDENCE

Those who can see God's hand in everything can best leave everything in God's hand.

(See: Assurance; Faith, Security, Trust)

CONFUSION

If you can keep your head in all this confusion, you simply don't know the situation.

CONSECRATION

D. L. Moody said he wanted the "O and O" degree—"Out and Out" for Jesus.

(See: Commitment, Surrender, Yieldedness)

CONTENTMENT

The richest person is the one who is contented with what he has.

If you cannot get what you like, why not try to like what you get?

Contentment makes poor men rich; Discontentment makes rich men poor.

(See: Satisfaction)

CONVICTIONS

Stand for something—or you'll fall for anything.

COOPERATION

As Christians, we should always work "heart to heart" even though we do not always see things "eye to eye."

Sometimes people are smart enough to realize it's easier to move a load by pulling together. We call that "horse sense."

COURAGE

What counts most is not the size of the dog in the fight, it's the size of the fight in the dog.

COURTESY

It's nice to be important, but it's more important to be nice.

(See: Kindness)

CREATION

Posterity will some day laugh at the foolishness of modern materialistic philosophy.

The more I study nature, the more I am amazed at the Creator. (Louis Pasteur)

CRIME

A great many people are worried about law and order. And a great many people are worried about justice. But one thing is certain—you cannot have either until you have both. (Ramsey Clark)

America is a nation where they lock up juries and let the criminals go out on the streets.

In America we'll try anything once—except criminals!

CRISIS

There is no such thing as a crisis with God. *We* are the ones always getting into jams. *We* are the "jammer-uppers."

CRITICISM

If you must publish someone's faults, then why not publish your own?

Many men who put antiknock in their automobiles, ought to take a dose of it themselves.

The man who rows the boat generally doesn't have time to rock it.

Remember, when you point your finger accusingly at someone else, you have three fingers pointing at yourself.

When I start to find fault
with all that I see,
It is time to start looking
for what's wrong with me.

A good way to avoid heart trouble:
—don't run upstairs, and
—don't run down people.

The most loved folks in our community seem to be the ones who never can recall anything bad about any of us.

(See: Complaining, Faultfinding, Grouchiness, Grumbling)

CURIOSITY

If you tell a man there are 300 billion stars in the universe, he'll believe you. But if you tell him a park bench has just been painted, he has to touch it to be sure.

Some folks aren't interested in anything unless it's none of their business.

There is only one fellow who doesn't mind if you stick your nose into his business—that's the guy who makes Kleenex!

DEATH

No one ever repented of being a Christian on his deathbed.

I am standing on the seashore. A ship spreads her white sails to the morning breeze and starts for the ocean. I stand watching her until she fades on the horizon, and someone at my side says, "She is gone."

Gone where? The loss of sight is in me, not in her. Just at the moment when someone says, "She is gone," there are others who are watching her coming. Other voices take up the glad shout, "Here she comes," and that is dying.
(Henry Scott Holland)

This isn't death I'm facing,
   but it's life forevermore.
It's not the end I'm nearing;
   it is entering heaven's door.
The way ahead is fairer
   than it's ever been before,
For it's *glory,* yes it's *glory*
   over yonder!
(H. H. Savage)

I am in perfect peace, resting alone on the blood of Christ. I find this amply sufficient with which to enter the presence of God. (Mel Trotter)

The sun is setting; mine is rising. I go from this bed to a crown. Farewell.
(S. B. Bangs)

The chariot has come, and I am ready to step in. (Margaret Prior)

This isn't death—it's glory;
It isn't dark—it's light.
It isn't stumbling, groping
    or even faith—it's sight!
It isn't grief—it's having
    the last tear wiped away;
It's sunrise, it's the morning
    of my eternal day!

Two fellows watched the funeral procession pass by—the richest man in town had died.
    "How much did he leave?" asked one.
    "He left it all," was the answer.
    We never see a hearse going to a cemetery with a U-Haul trailer behind it, loaded with the dead man's possessions. No man can take even his golf clubs with him.

When Tom Paine was dying he whispered, "I would give worlds, if I had them, if the *Age of Reason* had never been published. Oh Lord, help me! Christ, help me! It is hell to be left alone!"

Susie: "Why does your grandmother read
    the Bible so much in her old age?"
Jeannie: "I think it's because she's
    cramming for her final exams."

Let us endeavor so to live that when we
die even the undertaker will be sorry.
(Mark Twain)

Engraved on a tombstone:
"I expected this, but not just yet!"

Oftentimes we don't appreciate life until
it's time for it to end.

Life is a one way street—we are not
coming back.

Many who expect to be saved in the
eleventh hour, die at ten-thirty.

Found on a tombstone:
"I reveled underneath the moon,
I slept beneath the sun;
I lived a life of 'going to do,'
but died with nothing done."

All we can hold in our cold, dead hands
is what we have given away. (Old Sanskrit
proverb)

DECEIT

You may fool all the people some of the
time; you can even fool some of the
people all of the time; but you can't
fool all of the people all the time.
(Abraham Lincoln)

(We add—you cannot fool God any of the time.)

The easiest person to deceive is yourself.

(See: Falsehood, Honesty, Hypocrisy, Lying)

DELAYS

Let us not rebel against delay. We must not steal tomorrow out of God's hands. God is never too late. He is always right on time.

DECISIONS

When you don't know what next to do— don't do it!

DENTISTS

The favorite song of dentists is: "The Yanks Are Coming!"

DEPRESSION

When you are down in the mouth, remember Jonah. He came out all right.

Don't despair because you have occasional sinking spells of despondency —just remember the sun has a sinking spell every night.

DIETING

You can't reduce by talking about it. You have to keep your mouth shut!

DIFFICULTIES

If life gives you a lemon—just make it into *lemonade!*

I have suffered from being misunderstood, but I would have suffered more had I been understood. (Clarence Darrow)

If you find a path with no obstacles— it is probably a path that doesn't lead anywhere.

(See: Adversity, Burdens, Problems, Temptation, Trials)

DISAPPOINTMENT

Of all sad words of tongue or pen, the saddest are, "It might have been."

DISCIPLESHIP

Sonship costs us nothing,
Jesus paid the price.
Discipleship costs us all we have,
A total sacrifice.

DISCONTENT

Don't be a *cloud* because you failed to become a *star.*

DISCOURAGEMENT

Do not be discouraged—it may be the last key in the bunch that opens the door.

(See: Laziness, Perseverance, Stick-to-itiveness)

DISOBEDIENCE

If you go against the grain of God's laws, you get splinters!

DOCTORS

Never argue with the doctor—he has inside information!

DRIVING

Don't show off when driving. If you want to race—go to Indianapolis!

When driving your car, watch the car that is behind the car in front of you.

Always try to drive so that your license will expire before you do.

(See: Automobiles)

EATING

More people commit suicide with a knife, fork, and spoon than with any other weapon.

ECOLOGY

The ecologists are greatly concerned about the pollution in the air. Yes, but we aren't obliged to *listen* to it!

ECONOMICS

It would be a novelty to have this country's fiscal policy managed by someone who has been compelled to earn a living.

We owe a great deal to our forefathers, and that's another debt we will probably never repay.

Old accountants never die—they just lose their balance.

The modern way of doing things is: to drive a car that is still unpaid for, on an expressway that is bond-financed, using gasoline bought with a credit card.

(See: Finances, Money, Luxury, Stewardship, Treasures, Wealth)

EDUCATION

If you think education is expensive, try ignorance. (bumper sticker)

A hundred mistakes are an education if you learn something from each one.

Most people are willing to pay more to be amused than to be educated.

EFFECTIVENESS

If your efficiency doesn't have Christ's sufficiency, it will result in deficiency.

EGOTISM

Egotist: "I have many faults, but being wrong isn't one of them."

When two egotists meet, it is a case of an "I" for an "I."

His conversation was on a "boast-to-boast" network.

EMPLOYMENT

The man who knows *how* will find a job. The man who knows *why* will be his boss.

ENCOURAGEMENT

He who climbs the highest is he who helps another ascend.

The best thing to do behind a person's back—is pat it!

ENGAGEMENT

Getting engaged is: an urge on the verge of a merge.

ENVY

People who are green with envy are ripe for trouble.

ETERNITY

My interest is in the future because I am going to spend the rest of my life there. (C. F. Kettering)

He who provides for this life, but makes no provision for eternity, is wise for a moment, but a fool forever.

We humans make provision for this life as if it would never end, and we make provision for the life to come as if it would never begin.

We will have all eternity in which to celebrate our victories, but we have so little time left in which to win them.

EVOLUTION

First he was a pollywog—beginning to
    begin;
Then he was a froggy—with his tail tucked
    in;
Then he was a monkey—in a banyan tree;
Now he is a doctor—with a Ph.D!

The probability of life originating by
accident is comparable to the probability
of the unabridged dictionary resulting
from an explosion in the print shop.
(Edwin Conklin)

If you meet a fellow who claims he
descended from a monkey, don't argue
with him . . . because, after all, he knows
his family better than you do.

FAILURES

A man may make many mistakes, but he is not a failure until he starts blaming someone else for them.

Failures are divided into two categories:
—those who thought and never did, and
—those who did and never thought.

There is no failure more complete than the so-called success that leaves God out of the project.

Men who try something and fail are infinitely better than those who try nothing and succeed.

There is no such thing as failure inside the will of God. There is no such thing as real success outside the will of God.

(See: Mistakes, Right/Wrong, Success)

FAITH

The world says, "Seeing is believing."
Faith says, "Believing is seeing!"

It is faith alone that justifies, but faith that justifies can never be alone.
(John Calvin)

Faith is only as good as its object. The man in the jungle bows before an idol of stone and trusts it to help him, but he receives no help. If faith is not directed at the right object, it will accomplish nothing. The big question is, "In whom do you believe?"

Faith isn't believing in spite of evidence. Faith is obeying in spite of consequence.

Feed your faith and your doubts will starve to death.

Go as far as you can see. When you get there, you can see farther.

Little faith will bring us to heaven, but great faith will bring heaven to us.

(See: Assurance, Confidence, Doubts, Security, Trust, Works, Worry)

FALSEHOOD

The trouble with stretching the truth is that it is liable to snap back.

(See: Deceit, Honesty, Hypocrisy, Lying)

FAMILY

Since the coming of television we no longer have family circles—we have semi-circles.

It seems that almost every family tree has some sap in it.

The family that PRAYS together,
　　　　　　STAYS together.
The family that TALKS together,
　　　　　　WALKS together.
The family that SINGS together,
　　　　　　CLINGS together.

FAREWELLS

God's children never say good-bye for the last time.

FAULTFINDING

If you want to set the world right, start with yourself.

Putting your best foot forward doesn't mean to kick about everything.

When I start to find fault
　with all that I see,
It is time to start looking
　for what's wrong with me.

When looking for faults, use a mirror, not a telescope!

We should cover the faults of our fellow-workers with a cloak of charity, because we may need a circus tent to cover our own.

If you are looking for an easy project— try faultfinding. It requires no talent, no

brains, and no character to get started in
the business of grumbling.

(See: Complaining, Criticism,
Grouchiness, Grumbling)

FELLOWSHIP

There are three ways we can get together:
First—We can be like popcorn in a popper
and explode at each other.
Second—We can be like ice cubes in a
refrigerator and freeze together.
Third—We can be like a box of choco-
lates in the summer sun and melt
together.

If you think it doesn't pay to stick
together, consider the banana. As soon as
it leaves the bunch it gets skinned!

FINANCES

In our present condition, if someone
offers you the world on a silver platter—
take the platter.

Many people would not have such fat
wallets if they removed their credit cards.

One of life's *hardest* jobs is to keep up
the *easy* payments.

(See: Economics, Money, Luxury,
Treasures, Stewardship, Wealth)

FIRMNESS

The way to conjugate the verb
"to be firm":
I am firm.
You are obstinate.
He is pigheaded.

FISHING

A fish grows faster than anything living—
especially when a fisherman is describing
it.

FLATTERY

Most of us would rather be ruined by
flattery than edified by rebuke.

FOOLS

There are two kinds of fools: those who
can't change their opinions and those who
won't. (Josh Billings)

(See: Mind, Knowledge, Thinking,
Wisdom)

FORGETFULNESS

If we could forget our troubles as easily
as we forget our blessings, how different
things would be.

FORGIVENESS

Jesus was always the God of the *new
beginning* (no matter what the sin, background of failure).

Many rejoice in being forgiven by God, but they refuse to forgive others.

Forgiveness is not condoning the wrong.

FREEDOM

There are two kinds of freedom—the false and the true:
    The false freedom—where one is free to do what he likes, and
    The true freedom—where one is free to do what he ought.
(Charles Kingsley)

Only those who are *servants* of Christ are truly *free* (from sin).

Isn't it strange that men will fight for the right to say what they think . . . and then say so much without thinking?

FRIENDS

It is true that a man is known by the company he keeps. It is also true that a man is known by the company he keeps out of.

It is smart to pick your friends—but not to pieces.

He who would have friends must show himself friendly.

A true friend is one who knows all about you, and likes you just the same.

GENEROSITY

It's better to have a big heart than to own a big house.

GEOGRAPHY

One thing the discovery of the North Pole revealed is that there is nobody sitting on top of the world.

GIRLS

A recent survey indicates:
—eight out of ten adolescent American girls want to grow up like their mothers—*but* without doing any housework.
—94 percent of American girls from ages eleven to eighteen fully expect to get married someday, but only three percent have any plan of becoming full-time housewives.

GOD

Our heavenly Father never takes anything from his children unless he plans to give them something better. (George Müller)

One of the kindest things God ever did was to put a curtain over tomorrow!

When you have nothing left but God, then for the first time you become aware that God is enough.

Man proposes—but God disposes. (Thomas A. Kempis)

The promises of God are just as good as cash money—any day. (Billy Bray)

With God's strength *behind* you, his love *within* you, and his arms *underneath* you, you are more than sufficient for the days *ahead* of you.

Little is much if God is in it.

There is nothing you can do to make God love you more. There is nothing you can do to make God love you less. His love is unconditional, impartial, everlasting, infinite, perfect! (Richard C. Halverson)

(See: Lord Jesus, Relationship with God)

GOOD OLD DAYS
In the good old days, people quit spending when they ran out of money.

The good old days were when inflation was something you did to a balloon.

Usually the person who is continually talking about the "good old days" didn't do much for the Lord then, and isn't doing much for the Lord now.

GOOD WORKS

I wish people would give at least as much attention to deeds as they do to creeds.

GOSSIP

If you gossip and throw dirt, just remember, you are losing ground.

There are no idle rumors. Rumors are always busy.

(See: Mouths, Rumors, Talk, Tongues, Words)

GOVERNMENT

If America is not buried by Red Russia from without, we may be smothered by red tape from within. (Vance Havner)

GRACE

The truth of God's grace . . . humbles a man without degrading him, and . . . exalts a man without inflating him.

GRATITUDE

He who is thankful for *little* enjoys much.

A grateful mind is a great mind and a happy mind. (Thomas Secker)

(See: Appreciation, Praise, Thankfulness)

GREATNESS

A sign of greatness is to be able to laugh at yourself with others—and enjoy it as much as they do.

Great minds . . . discuss ideas.
Average minds . . . discuss events.
Small minds . . . discuss people.

Strong people make as many mistakes as weak people. The difference is that strong people admit their mistakes . . . laugh at them and . . . learn from them. That is how they became strong.
(Richard Needham)

When the going gets tough, the tough get going.

The man who is too big for a small job, is too small for a big job.

It is greatness to do little things well.

(See: Littleness, Humility)

GREED

Getting what they deserve doesn't satisfy many people.

GROWTH

In the Christian life there are many promotions in spiritual growth, but there is no graduation. (T. J. Bach)

GROUCHINESS

Every drugstore sells mouthwashes for sweetening the breath, but why don't they offer something for sour dispositions?

When you feel dog-tired at night, it may be because you growled all day.

The worst kind of air pollution is not smog, but rather a sour disposition.

(See: Complaining, Criticism, Fault-finding, Grumbling)

GUIDANCE

When you need guidance, get close to God and the nearer you are to him, the clearer everything will appear.

Many people fervently pray, "Oh, God, guide me"; then they grab the steering wheel.

HABITS

Bad habits are like a comfortable bed . . .
easy to get into, but hard to get out of.

HATE

If I really love God there are some things
I will have to hate.

HAPPINESS

It isn't your *position* that makes you
happy or unhappy, it's your *disposition*.

If you find happiness by hunting for it,
you will probably find it, as the old woman
did her spectacles—safe on your own
nose all the time. (Josh Billings)

God doesn't want his children to walk
around unhappy. He wants them to be
happy. I am convinced that there is just
one place where there is not any laughter
and that is hell. And I've made arrange-
ments to miss hell, so, . . .

The secret of a happy life is to delight
in duty. When duty becomes delight, then
burdens become blessings.
(Warren Wiersbe)

Since I have been converted, I am happier
when I am unhappy than when I used to
be happy before I was converted.
(John McNeil)

Happiness is something that multiplies
by division.

To find happiness, one must concern
himself with what he owes the world,
not with what the world owes him.

It is not doing the thing we like that
makes life happy; it is learning to like the
thing we have to do.

(See: Cheerfulness, Gratitude, Joy,
Smiles, Praise, Thankfulness)

HEALTH

Ulcers may be a blessing. Look how
they cut down on your food bill.

If we observe all the health hints these
days we must:
—eat what we don't like,
—drink what we don't want, and
—do what we'd rather not.

HEAVEN

The Lord has gone to prepare a place for us, and we must prepare ourselves for that place.

HELL

Oh that I could lie upon the fire that is never quenched for a thousand years (and thus) purchase the favor of God! But it is a fruitless wish. Millions of millions of years will bring me no nearer to the end of torments than one poor hour. Oh, eternity, eternity! For ever and for ever! Oh, the insufferable pangs of hell! (Francis Newport)

HEREDITY

The parents of bright children are strong believers in heredity.

HOLINESS

Lord, make me as holy as it is possible for an ex-sinner to be.

HOLY SPIRIT

Is the Holy Spirit only a *resident in* your life, or is he *president of* your life?

HOME

The man who cannot live for Christ in his home has no business giving a testimony for Christ in the church.

HONESTY

It is much better to suffer for the truth
than to be rewarded for a lie.
(Swedish proverb)

(See: Deceit, Falsehood, Hypocrisy, Lying)

HOSPITALITY

It is hard to make guests feel at home
when all the time you are wishing they
were.

HOW TO LIVE

There are four directions for the Christian
to look:
Look back—and praise him;
Look up—and trust him;
Look around—and serve him;
Look ahead—and expect him.

The horn that's tooting loudest is the one
that's in the fog.
(From an old sea captain's log)

To obtain God's best, we must give our
    best.
To win, we must surrender.
To live, we must die.
To receive, we must give.
(Oswald J. Smith)

Live in such a way that the preacher can
tell the truth at your funeral.

Do all the good you can,
By all the means you can,

In all the ways you can,
In all the places you can,
To all the people you can,
At all the times you can,
As long as ever you can.
(John Wesley)

Some people are so heavenly minded they are no earthly good.

I am ready to go anywhere—provided it be *forward*. (David Livingstone)

Live the life, if you are going to talk the talk.

Don't sacrifice the permanent on the altar of the immediate. (Bob Jones, Sr.)

The faith of some is a dead faith. Such people substitute words for deeds. They know the correct vocabulary for prayer and testimony—but their walk does not measure up to their talk. They think that their words are as good as works, and they are wrong. (Warren Wiersbe)

Under America's free-enterprise system, if at first you don't succeed you drop in another coin and kick the vending machine. (George Eyer)

One should give more concern to making a life than to making a living.

It is when we forget ourselves that we do things that will be remembered.

To rise to the top you must first get to the bottom of things.

Don't think you are necessarily on the right road because it is a well-beaten path.

A humble woman had this splendid philosophy:
"When I works—I works hard;
When I sits—I sits loose;
When I worries—bless your heart,
    I just falls to sleep."

One makes a living by what he gets; he makes a life by what he gives.

Jumping to conclusions is not nearly so good a mental exercise as digging for facts.

If you were on trial, accused of being a Christian, would there be enough evidence to convict you?

The way we behave toward people indicates what we really believe about God! (Warren Wiersbe)

Unless there is *within* us that which is *above* us, we shall soon yield to that which is *about* us.

So live, that as people get to know you better they will get to know Christ better.

Live each day as if it's your last—it may be.

I am not bound to win, but I am bound to
be true. I am not bound to succeed, but
I am bound to live up to the light I have.
I must stand with anybody who stands
for right:
—stand with him while he is right, and
—part with him when he goes wrong.
(Abraham Lincoln)

If you are the kind who wants just enough
Christianity to make you respectable; if
you merely want the name of Christian
without living the life; then you are a
disgrace to the Lord!

(See: Character, Conduct, Quarreling,
Relationship with Others)

HUMAN RACE
Nobody knows the age of the human race,
but all agree it is old enough to know
better.

HUMILITY
Humility is like underwear—essential,
but indecent if it shows.

The yoke of the Lord Jesus will never fit a
stiff neck.

The first test of whether a man is truly
great is an examination of his humility.

Those who have a right to boast, don't
need to.

It takes more grace than one can tell
to play the second fiddle well.

(See: Conceit, Pride, Self, Me-first)

HURRY

A man in Boston met a famous Chinese
scholar at the train station and imme-
diately rushed him toward the subway
station. The host panted to his guest, "If
we run and catch this next train, we will
save three minutes!"

To which the patient Chinese philoso-
pher replied, "And what significant thing
shall we do with the three minutes we are
saving?" (Warren Wiersbe)

The hurrier I go—the behinder I get.

(See: Patience)

HUSBANDS

Try praising your wife, even if it does
frighten her at first. (Billy Sunday)

Congratulations to the husband who
uncomplainingly observed that his wife's
constant chattering is just one of "life's
little *earitations*."

(See: Children, Family, Marriage, Parents,
Wives)

HYPOCRISY

The job many people spend most of their time at—is the job of hiding what they really are.

(See: Deceit, Falsehood, Lying)

IMPOSSIBILITIES

We are all faced with a series of great opportunities brilliantly disguised as impossible situations.
(Charles R. Swindoll)

INQUIRY

One who never asks questions either knows *everything* or *nothing*.
(Malcolm S. Forbes)

INSURANCE

With all of today's attractive accident policies, a man just can't afford to die a natural death.

INTERFERENCE

Some things come out better without our help . . . like a bud opening into a beautiful flower.

IRRITATIONS

People who tell you never to let little things bother you have never tried sleeping in a room with a mosquito. (Katherine Chandler)

You are only as big as the things that annoy you.

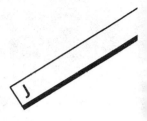

JESUS

Look at other people and you will be discouraged and disappointed; but look to Jesus and you will be blessed, satisfied, and transformed!

Look at yourself—and be disappointed;
Look at others—and be depressed;
Look at the Lord Jesus—and be satisfied.

Unless Jesus Christ is Lord of *all,* he cannot be Lord *at all.*

If you have Christ on the *inside,* you can stand up to any crisis on the *outside.*

Statesmanship and diplomacy have failed. The only remedy is Jesus Christ. It is either Christ or Chaos. (David Lloyd George, Prime Minister of England)

It will cost you your sins if you come to Jesus, but it will cost you your soul if you do not come to him. (Gypsy Smith)

It is out of order to invite the Lord Jesus into the parlor of our hearts if we entertain the devil in the cellar of our habits.

I have a great need for Christ.
I have a great Christ for my need!
(Charles H. Spurgeon)

If the Lord Jesus isn't worth serving every moment of every day, then he is not worth serving any moment of any day.

If the Lord Jesus is the center of my life, the circumference will take care of itself.

If Socrates would enter the room, we would rise and do him honor. But if Jesus Christ would come into the room, we should fall down on our knees and worship him. (Napoleon)

There are three possible positions the Lord Jesus can occupy in a Christian's life:
In all Christians, he is *present.*
In some Christians, he is *prominent.*
In a few Christians, he is *pre-eminent.*

Jesus will heal your wounded heart, if you give him all of it.

The Lord Jesus (who is God) became the Son of *man,* in order that I (a mere man) might become a son of *God!*

(See: Relationship with God)

JOB
Do you do your job each day well enough that you would hire yourself?

JOY

A hearty laugh and a sunny smile combine to produce the cheapest and best medicine known anywhere in the world.

If you don't enjoy what you have now, how can you be happier with more?

Those who have experienced the true joy of the Lord will never be satisfied with merely having fun.

The most miserable people in all the world are those who make pleasure a business.

If there is no sorrow for sin, there will be no joy in salvation.

A bitter world cannot be sweetened by sour Christians.

A rejoicing Christian is one of God's best advertisements.

If you want to be happy,
   begin where you are;
Don't wait for some rapture
   that's future and far.
Start now to be joyous;
   resolve to be glad;
And soon you'll forget that
   you ever were sad.

(See: Cheerfulness, Gratitude, Happiness, Praise, Smiles, Thankfulness)

JUDGING

Jumping to conclusions is not half as good exercise as digging for facts.

You and I have no business setting ourselves up as judges—unless we know all that God knows about people.

KINDNESS

If you are *unkind,* you are the *wrong kind!*

(See: Courtesy)

KNOWLEDGE

Any man who knows all the answers most likely misunderstood the questions.

The less a man knows the easier it is to convince him he knows it all.

(See: Fools, Mind, Thinking, Wisdom)

LAZINESS

Remember—even if you are on the right track, you'll get run over if you just sit there!

You can't leave your footprints on the sands of time while sitting down.

A very bad thing about loafing is I can't quit and rest!

A sign on the window of a bus station:
IF YOU HAVE NOTHING TO DO—
DON'T DO IT AROUND HERE!

Sitting still and wishing
   makes no person great;
The good Lord sends the fishing
   but you must dig the bait!

Nothing is more exhausting than searching for easy ways to make a living.

The new employee arrived late for work. His angry boss yelled, "You should have been here at eight!"

   "Why?" he asked, wide-eyed, "What happened?"

Many people are like a wheelbarrow—they go no further than they are pushed.

He who continually watches the clock need not worry about the future. He simply doesn't have any.

Old-man Lackadaisical: "Praise the blessed Lord for the nights in which to sleep—and the days in which to rest!"

The worst kind of fatigue is to be tired of doing nothing.

Rip Van Winkle is the only person who ever became famous while he was asleep.

There is nothing wrong with sleep . . . just don't overdo it.

(See: Lethargy, Perseverance, Uselessness)

LEADERSHIP

Avoid following the crowd.
Be an engine—not a caboose.

The concept many have of leadership is to observe which way the crowd is going—then grab a flag, run to the front of the gang, and yell, "I'm a leader! I'm a leader!"

Every business executive should sit back and meditate for a while each day—and try not to snore!

Those who are willing to face the music, may someday lead the band.

Remember the turtle—he never makes any progress until he sticks his neck out.

We herd sheep, drive cattle, and lead men.

If God has called you, do not spend any time looking over your shoulder to see who is following.

Blessed is the man who has learned to admire without envy, to follow without mimicking, to praise without flattery, and to lead without manipulation.

LEARNING

He who learns and learns
   but acts not what he knows,
Is like one who plows and plows,
   but never, never sows.

We should learn something every day. Sometimes it is the discovery that what we learned yesterday was wrong.

LETHARGY

If you want to get a pail of milk, don't sit yourself on a stool in the middle of a field hoping that a cow will come over to you.

Many Christians are not "standing on the promises"; they are just sitting on the premises. (Vance Havner)

(See: Laziness)

LIFE

We ought to do more with life than increase it's speed.

We can do little to *lengthen* our lives, but we can do much to *deepen* them and *broaden* them.

If life is a grind—use it to sharpen your wits.

LIQUOR

Statistics show that 10,000 people are killed by liquor for every person who is killed by a mad dog. So what do we do? We shoot the dog and license the liquor!

The four greatest scourges of mankind have been:
War
Drunkenness
Pestilence
Famine
And strong drink has been more destructive than war, pestilence, and famine combined. (William E. Gladstone)

(See: Alcohol)

LUXURY

The difference between a luxury and a necessity is—whether I have it or my friend has it.

(See: Money, Possessions, Wealth)

LYING

The worst lie is to lie to myself.
The worst deceit is to deceive myself.

A lie is a coward's way of getting out of trouble.

Mrs. Brown was shocked to learn that Johnny had told a lie. She took him to one side to graphically explain the consequences of falsehood,

"A tall, ugly man with red fiery eyes and two sharp horns grabs little boys who tell lies and carries them off at night. He takes them to Mars where they have to work in a dark canyon for fifty years. Now, Johnny, you'll never tell a lie again, will you?"

Johnny replied, "No, Mom—you tell better ones than I can."

Your income tax reveals two things: the amount of your income, and the amount of your honesty.

Those who tell white lies soon become color blind.

(See: Deceit, Falsehood, Honesty, Hypocrisy)

MARRIAGE

The goal in marriage is not to think alike, but to think together. (Robert C. Dodds)

Men and women chasing each other is what produces the human race. (Mark Beltaire)

Two love birds get together—and then come the little bills!

A young man's hardest problem is to find a girl attractive enough to please him, and dumb enough to marry him.

The cause of broken marriages is selfishness in one form or another.

Change one letter in the word "united" and it reads "untied." That letter is "I." (Vance Havner)

When I got married I closed the door to every other woman in the world; and since then I haven't even peeked through the keyhole. (Evangelist Sam Jones)

(See: Children, Family, Husbands, Parents, Wives)

MATHEMATICS

A lesson in mathematics:
A little sin will . . .
add to your trouble;
subtract from your energy; and
multiply your difficulties.

MATURITY

Few men ever grow up—they merely change their toys.

ME-FIRST

First—I come;
Then—I come again;
And you—you don't come for a long time.
(German saying)

Pyramid climbers are among us, not only in politics, industry and society, but also in the church.

Almost every church has its cliques, and often, new Christians find it difficult to get in.

Some church members use their offices to enhance their own images of importance. (Warren Wiersbe)

Some people conduct their lives on the cafeteria plan—self-service only.

(See: Conceit, Pride, Self)

MIDDLE AGE

There is now a new margarine on the market for people over forty. It is called "the middle-age spread."

Middle age is the time when a narrow waist and a broad mind change places.

MINDS

Vacant lots and vacant minds usually become dumping grounds for a lot of rubbish.

Many minds are like concrete—all mixed up and permanently set.

My mind is already made up—don't confuse me with the facts.

A great many so-called "open minds" should be closed for repairs.

You never can be quite sure what kind of mind a person has until he gives you a piece of it.

(See: Fools, Knowledge, Thinking, Wisdom)

MISSIONS

There is a mighty "go" in the word "gospel."

To love the whole world for me is no chore. My tough problem's the neighbor next door.

Many people give to missions merely as a sense of duty, like a divorced man paying alimony.

To every lost soul Christ says, "Come unto me."
To every saved soul Christ says, "Go for me."

Many young men who should say, "Here am I, Lord, send me," change it to, "Here am I, Lord, send my sister."

As the missionary offering was being received the usher approached a wealthy man and held out the plate. The rich man shook his head saying in a whisper, "I never give to missions."

The usher replied, "Then take something out—this money is for the heathen!"

MISTAKES

The greatest of all faults is to imagine you have none.

Things could be worse—suppose your errors were published every day like those of baseball players?

There's an old saying, "Erasers are for people who make errors."

A better expression is, "Erasers are for people who are willing to correct their mistakes!"

Learn from the mistakes of others. You won't live long enough to make them all yourself.

The fellow who will never admit he was wrong really is saying he is no smarter now than he used to be.

To make mistakes is human.
To repeat old mistakes is stupid.

We all make mistakes—that's why they put rubber mats under cuspidors.

The main difference between the wise man and a fool is that a fool's mistakes never teach him anything.

To err is common and normal.
To admit it is very unlikely.

A mistake, if understood, is but a step toward wisdom.

(See: Failure)

MODERN TIMES

Our food is synthetic;
Our faces cosmetic;
Our clothing pathetic, and
Our religion dyspeptic.
(Charles F. Taylor)

MONEY

If money is all you want, money is absolutely all you'll get.

It's great to be able to make both ends meet—but it's even better if they overlap just a little!

The hardest kind of money to get is— enough.

It is unfortunate to have more dollars than sense.

It isn't what you have in your pocket that makes you thankful, but what you have in your heart.

You can't take your money to heaven with you . . . but you can send it on ahead.

If you put money in the bank, *it* grows . . . put it in the offering plate and *you* grow.

It's tough to be poor . . . but not as bad as being in debt.

The real measure of a man's worth is— how much would he be worth if he lost all his money?

When your *outgo* exceeds your *income,* your *upkeep* causes your *downfall.*

A good analysis of our finances is not how much of *my* money do I give to God, but how much of *God's* money do I keep for myself.

Aren't people ridiculous? They spend money they don't have, to buy things they don't need, to impress folks they don't like.

That money talks—is plain to see;
It always says, "Good-bye" to me.

A minister when announcing the offering
said: "And now, brethren, let us all give
in accordance with what we reported on
our income tax."

Someone asked the famous millionaire,
John D. Rockefeller, "How much money
is enough, Mr. Rockefeller?"
   With a twinkle in his eye he answered,
"Always a little bit more."

The reason a young man leaves the farm
to work in the city is to make enough
money to retire and move back on a farm.

In the old days, a man who saved his
money was called a miser. Nowadays he is
called an amazing wonder.

When it comes to giving, some people
stop at nothing!

A fool and his money are soon invited
places.

(See: Economics, Finances, Luxury,
Stewardship, Treasures, Wealth)

MOON
Getting to the moon is becoming easier
all the time. It's staying on earth that is
becoming difficult.

MOTHERS

An ounce of mother is worth a pound
of preacher.

Garth: "Which of the translations of the
Bible do you like best?"
Al: "I like the version according to
mother."

MOUTHS

Nothing is more frequently "opened by
mistake" than the mouth.

Lord, fill my mouth
with worthwhile stuff,
And nudge me when
I've said enough.

El pez por su boca muere. (The fish dies
because of its mouth.) (Spanish proverb)

(See: Gossip, Rumors, Talk, Tongues,
Words)

MUSIC

"Out of the mire—and into the choir"
is the result of this great salvation.
(See Psalm 40:2, 3)

Sometimes B sharp;
Never B flat;
Always B natural.

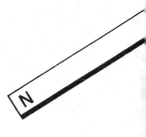

NEW YEAR

There are four ways to face the New Year:
... Some do it with —*hangover*
... Some face it with—*horror*
... Some face it with a—*hush*
... Others enter it with a—*heavenly hallulujah.*

NUTS

Testimony of an enthusiastic Christian:
"If people want to call me a nut, that's OK. But remember, I'm screwed on to a strong bolt!"

OLD AGE

As soon as you feel too old to do a thing
—*do it!* (Margaret Deland)

As we grow older, let's become more like
a peach *inside*, and less like a prune
outside.

Old age can't seem to catch up with folks
who have more things to do than they can
possibly finish.

Much more important than adding years
to your life, is to add life to your years.

Don't just grow old—grow up!

They can't call you an old dog as long as
you are learning new tricks.

A fellow celebrating his 100th birthday
was asked if he had some observation to
share.
   He answered, "Well, if I had known I was
going to live so long, I would have taken
better care of myself!"

The best thing about growing old is that
it takes such a long time.

Hardening of the heart ages people more quickly than hardening of the arteries.

By the time a man finds greener pastures, he can't climb the fence.

(See: Age, Middle Age, Talk, Tongues, Words)

OPPORTUNITY

Great opportunities come to those who make the most of small ones.

You never get a second chance to make a good first impression.

When opportunity knocks, some people object to the noise!

There is only one endeavor in which you can start at the top and that's digging a hole!

OPTIMIST

An optimist is one who thinks the preacher is nearly finished when he says, "Finally . . ."

An optimist defines a window as something to let light shine through.
    A pessimist defines a window as something that gets dirty and needs washing.

(See: Pessimist, Cheerfulness, Joy)

OUTLOOK

When the outlook is bad, try the *up-look.*

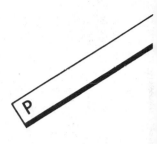

PARENTS

Oftentimes when we hear our children talk, we realize we should have been more careful of what they heard us say.

The best inheritance a parent can give his children is—a few minutes of his time each day.

A dad reprimanded his boy for not doing his homework. "What do you think Abraham Lincoln was doing when he was your age?"
   Son: "I don't know, but I do know what he was doing when he was *your age*."

Bring up a child in the way he should go, and go that way yourself.

There are too many dads who will tie up the dog at night and let their sons run loose.

Don't let your parents down—remember, they brought you up.

91

Parents can tell but never teach,
Until they practice what they preach.

Too many parents are not on speaking
terms with their children.

(See: Children, Family, Husbands,
Marriage, Wives)

PAST

An old proverb declares, "Dwell on the
past and you'll lose an eye; forget the
past and you'll lose both eyes."

PATIENCE

The American's prayer:
"Lord, give me patience, and I want it
right now!"

How can a society that exists on
—instant mashed potatoes,
—packaged cake mixes,
—frozen dinners, and
—instant cameras
teach patience to its young?
(Paul Sweeney)

Wouldn't it be wonderful if men would
show as much patience with their wives
and kids as they do when waiting for a
fish to bite?

(See: Hurry)

PERSEVERANCE

It is always too soon to quit.

A teacher lecturing on perseverance said: "He drove straight to his goal. He looked neither to the right nor to the left, but pressed forward, moved by a definite purpose. Neither friend nor foe could delay him, nor turn him from his course. What would you call such a man?" Student: "A truck driver!"

When it is definitely settled by a committee that a thing can't be done, watch somebody go ahead and do it.

(See: Stick-to-itiveness, Patience)

PLANNING

People don't plan to fail—they just fail to plan.

PLEASURE

All of us can bring pleasure in some way. Some bring pleasure by coming into the room; others by going out.

There's nothing wrong with living a life of pleasure . . . if we get pleasure out of the right things.

POLITICS

Political bumper stickers often last longer than the politicians.

POPULARITY

Do not weaken your spiritual power by a passion for popularity. (T. J. Bach)

POSITIVE THINKING

A good thing to remember,
  and a better thing to do;
Is to work with the construction gang
  and not the wrecking crew.

POSSIBILITIES

Longfellow could take a worthless piece of
paper, write a poem upon it and make it
worth $6,000—that is *genius.*

Rockefeller can sign his name to a
piece of paper and make it worth millions
—that is *capital.*

A mechanic can take material worth $5
and make an article worth $50—that is
skill.

An artist can take a 50 cent piece of
canvas, paint a picture on it and make it
worth a $1,000—that is *art.*

God can take a worthless, sinful life,
wash it in the blood of Christ, put his
Spirit in it, and make it a blessing to
humanity—that is *salvation.*

PRACTICE WHAT YOU PREACH

A pint of example is worth a gallon of
advice.

PRAISE

To praise God for our miseries—ends
them. To praise God for our blessings—
extends them.

(See: Appreciation, Gratitude, Joy,
Thankfulness)

PRAYER

You will not stumble while on your knees.

Why pray when you can worry?

The purpose of prayer is not to get *man's* will done in heaven, but to get *God's will* done on earth. (Warren Wiersbe)

Nothing lies beyond the reach of prayer except that which lies outside the will of God.

It is as natural for the spiritual man to pray as it is for the natural man to breathe.

Prayer is asking for rain.
Faith is carrying the umbrella.

The truest economy of time and labor is to be found in prayer.
The quickest way to solve any problem is to first bathe it in prayer.

A good prayer:
"O God, grant me the serenity to accept the things I cannot change, the courage to change the things I can, and the wisdom to know the difference."
(Reinhold Niebuhr)

If you find it hard to *stand* for Jesus, try kneeling first.

A bent knee makes a strong back.

The prayer of a Sioux Indian:
"Great Spirit, help me never to judge

another until I have walked two weeks in
his moccasins."

Prayerless pews make powerless pulpits.

God will not accept praying as a substitute for obeying.

People who do a lot of kneeling don't do
much lying.

A wise man's prayer:
"O God, give the world common sense,
beginning with me."

Sinning stops praying and . . .
Praying stops sinning.

Do not face the day until you have faced
God.

I wonder if the men who pray so piously
in our church ever try using the same tone
of voice when talking to a neighbor or
to the fellow who bumped into his car.

One day of preaching (Day of Pentecost)
was preceded by ten days of praying.
Our pattern is oftentimes—one day of
praying precedes ten days of preaching.

PREACHERS

Preachers should go out to feed the
sheep not amuse the goats. (R. A. Torrey)

Some preachers evidently feel that when
truth was being distributed by the Lord,
they got most of it. (Wayne Hoehns)

Candles on the altar of a church will never be a substitute for a flame in the pulpit.

The degree of welcome for a preacher in some homes depends upon how sick somebody is.

Many folks aren't much interested in preachers until there is a death in the family.

If you are strong on facts and weak on logic, talk facts.
If you are strong on logic and weak on facts, talk logic.
If you are weak on both logic and facts, POUND ON THE PULPIT!

Many preachers, in preparing their sermons, never prepare a place to stop.

Advice to preachers:
Put more fire into your sermons or put more sermons into the fire.
(Vance Havner)

To me, no sermon is really worthwhile unless I can hear the heartbeat.
(Henry W. Longfellow)

The finest compliment you can pay the sermon is to bring a friend to hear the next one.

PREJUDICES
It is never too late to give up your prejudices.

97

PREPARATION

I will study and get ready, and maybe my chance will come. (Abraham Lincoln)

PRIDE

There's not much sense keeping your nose to the grindstone just to turn it up at the neighbors.

The man who continually looks down his nose at others usually has the wrong slant.

The bigger a man's head gets, the easier it is to fill his shoes.

He who will not be counseled cannot be helped.

People who have grandiose ideas about how to run the world ought to start with a small garden. (Lou Erickson)

It is OK to hold up your head, just so you don't turn up your nose.

(See: Conceit, Humility, Me-first, Self)

PROBLEMS

It is too bad people can't exchange problems with each other, for all of us claim we know how to solve the other fellow's problem.

When going through problems or trials this motto is good:
"Try Thanksgiving"

The best way to forget your own problem is to help someone else solve his.

Are you contributing to the solution? Or are you a part of the problem?

(See: Difficulties, Trials)

PSYCHOLOGY

A new branch of psychology is called Psycho-Ceramics. It is a study of crack-pots!

Psychologists tell us that it is detrimental to be an orphan; a disadvantage to be the only child; crushing to be the middle child; and taxing to be the oldest child. Obviously, the only way out of the dilemma is to be born an adult!

A *normal* person is one who thinks two and two are four and accepts it.

A *psychotic* person is one who thinks two and two are five and believes it.

A *neurotic* person is one who thinks two and two are four and it bothers him.

PUNCTUALITY

The trouble with being punctual is that nine times out of ten there is nobody there to appreciate it.

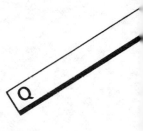

QUARRELS

The person who uses the loudest voice is the one who has the weakest argument.

Let's learn the lesson that we "can disagree without being disagreeable."

(See: Relationship with others)

QUITTERS

The only thing worse than a quitter is the man who is afraid to begin.

A quitter never wins and a winner never quits.

Be sure you're wrong before you quit.

(See: Perseverance)

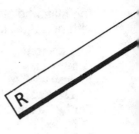

REFORMATION

Whitewashing the pump won't make the water pure. (Dwight L. Moody)

RELATIONSHIP WITH GOD

One plus the Lord = a majority.
One plus God = TRIUMPH!

If you are not living as close to God as you once did, you need not guess who moved.

To look around—is to be distressed.
To look within—is to be depressed.
To look to God—is to be blessed.

Lord, be *within me*—to strengthen me;
   without me—to preserve me;
   over me—to shelter me;
   beneath me—to support me;
   before me—to direct me;
   behind me—to bring me back;
   around me—to fortify me.
(Lancelot Andrews)

The man who puts God *first* will find God with him right up to the *last*.

To a computer—I am just another number.
To Jesus—I am an object of his fathomless love.
I'm just a small number, computers can trace;
But Christ knows my heartaches, my name and my face!

When God measures a man, he puts a tape around his heart—not his head!

When the Lord Jesus has *you* for anything, then you have *him* for *everything*.

Some folks are like the fifth carbon copy of the Lord Jesus Christ. There is so much between them and the Lord that the impression is very light indeed.

If God is your partner . . . make your plans BIG.

God is *for* us—that is good.
God is *with* us—that is better.
God is *in* us—that is best.

Nothing is more dreadful for a sinner nor more wonderful for a Christian than to be alone with God.

The secrets of the Lord are for those who live close to him.

There are no losers with Jesus and no winners with the devil. (Brandt)

Many Christians look upon the will of God as bitter medicine they must take, instead of seeing it as the gracious evidence of the love of God. (Warren Wiersbe)

Some people think God's will is a cold, impersonal machine. God starts it going and it is up to us to keep it functioning smoothly.

No, not at all! The will of God is a living relationship between God and the believer. When you and I get out of God's will, God adjusts things to bring us back into his will. (Warren Wiersbe)

The will of God will never lead you where the grace of God cannot keep you.

(See: God, Jesus)

RELATIONSHIP WITH OTHERS

The fellow who's on his toes doesn't usually have any trouble keeping other people from stepping on them.

The sins of other people are like the headlights of an oncoming car—they always seem more glaring than your own.

Men with clenched fists cannot shake hands.

With malice toward none, with charity for all, with firmness in the right. . . . (Abraham Lincoln)

It is pseudo-Christianity for a Christian
to love sinners and fight the saints.

A good suggestion for managers,
marriage partners—in fact for all of us:
    If you are willing to give way in little
things, you can almost always have your
way in big ones. (Sydney J. Harris)

Our faults irritate us most when we see
them in others.
(Proverb of the Pennsylvania Dutch)

See what you can do for others; not just
what *they* can do for you.

When you try to make an impression—
that is precisely the impression you make.

While seeking happiness for others we
unconsciously find it for ourselves.

To handle yourself . . . use your head.
To handle others . . . use your heart.

To return evil for good is . . devilish;
To return good for good is . . . neighborly;
To return good for evil is . . . godlike.

Don't worry about what people think
about you—the chances are they seldom
think about you at all.

When you open the window yourself,
    you get fresh air.
When someone else opens it,
    you get a draft.
(Lucille J. Goodyear)

You can't hold another fellow down in the ditch unless you stay down there with him. (Booker T. Washington)

(See: How to Live, Quarrels)

REST

Jesus knows we must come apart and rest awhile, or else we may just plain come apart! (Vance Havner)

REVENGE/VINDICTIVENESS

If revenge is sweet, why does it leave such a bitter taste?

REWARDS

He who lives for God's honor and glory seeks neither praise nor reward, but in the end he is certain of both.

RIGHT/WRONG

The crowd is usually going the wrong way. Sacred and secular history indicate that it is usually God's righteous minority bucking the crowd that is going the right way.

And now among the fading embers, these
    are my principal regrets:
When I am right—no one remembers;
When I am wrong—no one forgets.

(See: Failures, Mistakes, Success)

RESISTANCE

The way of least resistance usually goes downhill.

It seems as though I can resist everything —except temptation!

ROMANCE

The great drawback to a budding love affair is the blooming expense!

RUMORS

A rumor is like a check—don't endorse it until you are sure it's genuine.

Beware of a half-truth—you may have gotten the wrong half.

(See: Gossip, Mouths, Talk, Tongues, Words)

SAINTS

How lamentable is the way we praise the dead saints and persecute the living ones!

Instead of being "Latter Day Saints" why not be "Every Day Saints"?

SALVATION

There is a tremendous contrast between religion and salvation:
Religion is man trying to reach up to God.
Salvation is God reaching down to man.

God can save from the guttermost to the uttermost. (William Ward Ayer)

SATAN

The devil's number one strategy is to get you to procrastinate.

Satan is to be avoided as a lion, dreaded as a serpent, and most, to be feared as an angel of light!

There is one characteristic of the devil we ought to emulate—his persistance and stick-to-itiveness.

SATISFACTION

Try to be satisfied with your lot, even if you don't have a lot.

(See: Contentment)

SCHOOL

What most kids object to about school is the principal of the thing.

SECOND COMING

To be ready for the Lord's coming is a *necessity*. To deny the Lord's coming is *heresy*. To fix a date for his coming is *lunacy*.

Many people who believe in the second coming of Christ are secretly hoping he won't come today.

SECURITY

We may tremble on the Rock, but the Rock never trembles under us.

It is far safer to be in the storm *with* Christ, then to be in still water *without him.*

It is more secure to be on the front line of the battlefield *with* Christ, than to be seated in your living room *without* him.

Speaking of bomb shelters . . . how sad is the man whose only shelter is a hole in the ground.

(See: Assurance, Confidence, Faith, Trust)

SELF

Fortune smiles upon the person who can laugh at himself.

If you could kick in the pants the fellow responsible for most of your troubles, you wouldn't be able to sit down for six weeks.

Talk to a man about himself and he will be glad to listen for hours.

Whatever you may be sure of, be sure of this—you are dreadfully similar to other people.

We ask God to provide for our needs, and when he does, we congratulate ourselves on our ability and cleverness.

A man wrapped up in himself makes a very small package.

Just let a man talk about himself and he will think it's a mighty interesting conversation.

I have never met a man who has given me as much trouble as myself.
(Dwight L. Moody)

There is hope for any man who can look in the mirror and laugh at what he has seen.

(See: Conceit, Me-first, Pride)

SELF-CENTEREDNESS

"We've been talking too much about me. Now let's talk about you. What do *you* think of me?"

SEMINARS

It is easier to organize a conference on the quality of the environment than to stoop over and pick up a gum wrapper. (Bill Vaughan)

SERVICE

I am only one—but I am one.
I cannot do everything—but I can do
    something.
What I can do—I ought to do.
What I ought to do—I will do.

Everyone can do something to make the world better—he can at least improve himself.

Vision isn't enough—it must be combined with venture. It is not enough to stare up the steps—we must step up the stairs! (Vance Havner)

(See: Work, Zeal)

SIN

Sinful pleasures can make you laugh, but they can never dry your tears.

The *pleasures* of sin are "for a season," but the *wages* of sin are "for eternity."

Some people *confess* their faults—that's biblical.
Others *caress* them—that's sinful.

The trouble with a little sin is that it won't stay little.

Sin produces a moment of gratification and an eternity of remorse.

The Bible teaches that "the wages of sin is death."
Thank God I quit before payday.

If a Christian sins because Satan deceives him, that is bad. But if he sins because he has deceived himself, that is worse.

If you don't want the fruits of sin, stay out of the devil's orchard!

SINNER

A sinner . . . lives in sin and loves it;
A saint . . . lapses in sin and loathes it.

The way of the transgressor may be hard—but it isn't lonesome.

SLEEP

Speaking of tranquilizers—way back in Grandpa's day there was something to produce a good night's sleep. They called it work.

SMILES

Smiles never go up in price or down in value.

You can acquire a pleasant smile without going to the beauty shop.

It has been said that a smile adds a lot to your face value.

(See: Cheerfulness, Happiness, Joy)

SMUGNESS

To be complacently satisfied with yourself is a sure sign that progress is about to end.

SOUL-WINNERS

Talk to the Lord about sinners—then talk to sinners about God.

The greatest crime of the desert is to know where water is and not to tell about it. (Mildred Cable)

If we would win some to Christ we must be *winsome*.

Soul-winners are not soul-winners because of *what* they know, but because of *whom* they know, how *well* they know Him, and how much they long for others to know Him. (Dawson Trotman)

(See: Witnessing)

SPEED

We are now moving forward with twice the speed of sound and half the speed of sense. (Thomas Griffith)

SPIRITUAL GROWTH

For spiritual growth, it is not so much a question of *where I am,* but rather *what I am* where I am. (T. J. Bach)

SPORTS

We'll be in trouble as long as we pay the best professors less than the worst football coach.

STATUS QUO

Our dilemma is that we hate change, but we love it at the same time. What we really want is for things to remain the same but get better. (Sydney J. Harris)

STEWARDSHIP

Give according to your income, lest God make your income according to your giving.

You cannot outgive God.

Do your giving while you're living, Then you're knowing where it's going.

The average person hasn't stored up enough treasure in heaven to make a down payment on a harp.

I have held many things in my hands and have lost them. But whatever I have placed in God's hands, that I still possess. (Martin Luther)

A man had a dream in which God said to him, "I have decided how much your income will be each week. I will observe how much you place on the offering plate and then I will provide for you an income of exactly ten times that amount."

(See: Economics, Finances, Luxury, Money, Treasures, Wealth)

STICK-TO-ITIVENESS

Be like a postage stamp—it sticks to one thing until it gets the job done!

The smartest person is not the one who is quickest to *see through* a thing, rather it is the person who will *see a thing through.*

Tough times never last . . . but tough people do! (Robert Schuller)

(See: Patience, Perseverance)

SUCCESS

If you want to get a true estimate of a man, observe what he does when he has nothing to do.

Most of us would rather be ruined by flattery than to be benefitted by criticism.

Success is not attained by lying awake at night, but by staying awake in the day-time.

A valuable measure of success or failure is whether the tough problem you are facing is the same problem you had a year ago.

Remember, success comes in "cans," failures comes in "can'ts."

There are many roads to success—but they are all uphill.

If at first you don't succeed—you are about average.

Behind every successful man stands a loyal wife—and a surprised mother-in-law.

Those who never succeed themselves are always first to tell you how.

(See: Failures)

SUFFERING
It's no fun to suffer in silence unless you first make enough noise to attract attention and sympathizers.

SUPERIORITY COMPLEX
It is rather ridiculous to think we are better than Grandpa and Grandma simply because we have better and shinier gadgets.

SYMPATHY
No doctor is a good doctor who has never been ill himself. (Confucius)

TALK

He is breathtaking. Every few hours
he stops talking and takes a breath.

Generally speaking—he is generally
speaking.

It is good to have a train of thought—
provided you have a caboose to hitch on
to it.

No one wants to listen to you talk, unless
he believes it will be his turn next.

He who thinketh by the inch, and talketh
by the yard, ought to be dealt with by the
foot!

There is a vast difference between having
to say something and having something
to say.

It is much better to "walk your talk,"
than to "talk your walk."

As a man grows wiser, he talks less and
says more.

We must never be silent when we ought to speak. We must never speak when we ought to be silent.

If some of us practiced all we preach, we'd work our fool selves to death.

The trouble with a fellow who talks too fast is that he is apt to say things he hasn't even thought of yet.

God gave us two ears and only one mouth, which indicates we should listen twice as much as we talk.

The most boring people I've met are those who can think of nothing to talk about . . . and do it.

If you must speak your mind, then mind how you speak.

(See: Gossip, Mouths, Rumors, Tongues, Words)

TEARS

When our eyes are washed with tears, they can better see the invisible land where there shall be no more tears.

Strong men are those who can be brought to tears by God's love.

TEMPER

Before you give somebody a piece of your mind, be sure you can get by with what you have left!

You can't get rid of your temper by losing it.

Temper is such a valuable thing, it is a shame to lose it!

The more often you lose your temper, the more you have it.

A temper is a valuable possession, so *don't lose it!*

Nothing cooks your goose more quickly than a boiling temper.

When you are right, you can afford to keep your temper. When you are wrong, you can't afford to lose it.

(See: Anger)

TEMPTATION

When you meet temptation, always turn to the right.

When you flee temptation, be sure you don't leave a forwarding address.

(See: Difficulties, Trials)

TENDERNESS

Remember to keep your hearts tender toward the Lord and toward each other. (Nancy Woolnough)

THANKFULNESS

The words "think" and "thank" come from the same Latin root.

If we take the time to *think* more we will undoubtedly *thank* more.

(See: Cheerfulness, Gratitude, Joy, Praise)

THINKING

You are not what you think you are, but what you think, you are.

You cannot stop people from thinking . . . the job is to get some people started.

When you stop to think, don't forget to start again.

Some people become lost in thought because it is such unfamiliar territory to them.

You can do better than you think.
You can do better if you think.
You can do better—don't you think?

He who will not reason—is a bigot;
He who cannot reason—is a fool;
He who dares not—is a slave.
(William Drummond)

(See: Mind, Knowledge, Wisdom)

TIME

You cannot kill time without injuring eternity.

If you must kill time, why not try to work it to death?

You wake up in the morning and lo, your purse is magically filled with a treasure —of twenty-four hours.

It is yours—a priceless possession.

No one can take it from you.

And no one receives either more or less than you receive. (Arnold Bennett)

TOBACCO

Tobacco is a filthy weed,
   and from the devil doth proceed;
Robs your pockets—burns your clothes,
   and makes a chimney of your nose.

TODAY

Yesterday is gone;
Tomorrow is uncertain;
Today is here.
So *use* it!

TOLERANCE

The test of tolerance comes
   when we are in a majority.
The test of courage comes
   when we are in a minority.

TOMORROW

Tomorrow is the busiest day of the week.

The best preparation for tomorrow is the right use of today.

Tomorrow isn't likely to be much fun for the fellow who couldn't find anything to enjoy today.

TONGUES

So often the first screw that gets loose in a person's head is the one that holds the tongue in place.

Do be careful—remember your tongue is in a wet place and is apt to slip.

A dog has many friends because the wag was put in his tail, not his tongue.

En boca cerrada no entran moscas.
(A closed mouth doesn't catch flies.)
(Spanish proverb)

We can read some people like a book, but we can't shut them up as easily!

One may have false teeth, but let everyone have a true tongue.

The only bit that will bridle the tongue is a little bit of love.

The most untameable thing in the world has its den just back of your teeth.

A sharp tongue is no indication of a keen mind.

(See: Gossip, Mouths, Rumor, Talk, Words)

TRIALS

Let's learn a lesson from tea. It shows its real worth when it gets into hot water.

There are very few gains without pains . . . and very few triumphs without trials. There is no sunshine without shadows.

Scars are the price of scepters. Grief has always been the lot of greatness.

We are God's jewels. Often God exhibits his jewels on a dark background . . . so they will shine more brightly.

Nothing shows more accurately what kind of a Christian we really are than the way in which we meet trials and difficulties.

Be confident of this—if God sends you on stony paths, he will provide you with strong shoes.

The brook would lose its song if you removed the rocks and stones.

God's love does not always keep us *from* trials, but it is a love that always keeps us *through* trials.

There can be no victories without battles. There can be no peaks without valleys. There can be no roses without thorns.

The darkest hour has only sixty minutes.
(Morris Mandel)

Only with cutting and polishing is the
   beauty of the diamond produced.
Only with trials and testing is the beauty
   of Jesus produced in the Christian.

All sunshine makes a desert.
(Arab proverb)

(See: Adversity, Burdens, Difficulties,
Problems, Temptation)

TROUBLES

There is only one person who likes to hear
about your troubles—your lawyer. He gets
paid for it!

TRUST

Trust him—when dark days assail you;
Trust him—when your faith is small.
Trust him—when to simply trust him is
   the hardest thing of all.

Never be afraid to trust an unknown future
to a known God.

"Trust and OK," was the way one boy sang
the gospel song.

(See: Assurance, Confidence, Faith,
Security)

TRUTH

Truth needs no crutches.
If it limps, it's a lie!

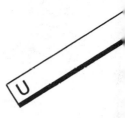

UNSELFISHNESS

Do unto others as though you were the others.

URGENCY

Do it *now!* Today will be yesterday tomorrow.

USELESSNESS

Sadder than work left unfinished is work never begun.

There are two kinds of people who never amount to much: those who can't do what they are told, and those who can do nothing else.

(See: Laziness, Lethargy)

VINDICTIVENESS

The only people with whom you should try to get even are those who have helped you.

VICE

The more a man is addicted to vice, the less he cares for advice.

WEALTH

A man's bank account doesn't indicate whether he is rich or poor. It is the heart that makes a man rich.

A man is rich according to what he *is,* not according to what he *has.*
(Henry Ward Beecher)

When a man becomes wealthy the important question is:
"Will God gain a fortune or lose a man?"

(See: Economics, Finances, Luxury, Money, Stewardship, Treasures)

WISDOM

It is good to be wise, and wise to be good.

A wise man thinks what he says; a fool says what he thinks.

Coldhearted intellectualism and hot-headed ignorance are both damaging to the cause of Christ.

He is a wise man who knows what *not* to say.

He is no fool who gives what he cannot keep, to gain what he cannot lose.
(Jim Elliot)

Wisdom is fortified, not destroyed, by understanding its limitations.
(Mortimer J. Adler)

Some folks are wise and some are otherwise.

Man's wisdom comes from reason.
God's wisdom comes from revelation.
(Warren Wiersbe)

The brain is no stronger than its weakest *think*.

The greatest undeveloped territory in all the world lies under your hat.

(See: Fools, Mind, Knowledge, Thinking)

WITNESSING

I'm just a *nobody* telling *anybody* about *somebody* who can save *everybody!*

It is imperative that I witness to unsaved souls about Jesus Christ.
    It is also imperative that the unsaved souls can see Jesus Christ in me.

(See: Soul-Winners)

WIVES/WOMEN

A woman's work is never done—especially if she asks her husband to do it.

You should never criticize your wife's judgment—look who she decided to marry!

A good woman inspires a man.
A brilliant woman interests a man.
A beautiful woman fascinates a man.
But it's the sympathetic woman who gets
    him.

Someone has said, "A woman's tears are the greatest water power known on earth."

(See: Children, Family, Husbands, Marriage, Parents)

WORDS

A careless word—may kindle strife,
A cruel word—may wreck a life,
A bitter word—may hate instill,
A brutal word—may smite and kill.
A gracious word—may smoothe the way,
A joyous word—may light the day.
A timely word—may lessen stress,
A loving word—may heal and bless.
(The War Cry)

A wise old owl sat in an oak;
    The more he saw the less he spoke;
The less he spoke the more he heard.
    Why can't we be like that old bird?

The man who has to eat his own words never asks for a second helping.

If a thing will go without saying—then
let it go!

Sharp words will upset the stomach,
especially if you have to eat them.

He has an uncanny ability for compressing
a minimum of thought into a maximum
of words.

When there's nothing more to be said,
he is still saying it.

I try to watch the words I say,
    and keep them soft and sweet.
For I don't know from day to day
    which ones I'll have to eat.

(See: Gossip, Mouths, Rumor, Talk,
Tongues)

WORK

Follow the example of the duck—keep
calm and unruffled on the surface, but
paddle like the dickens underneath.

Many people avoid discovering the secret
of success because deep down they
suspect the secret may be—*hard work!*

I do not pray for a lighter load, but
for a stronger back. (Phillips Brooks)

After all is said and done, there is much
more said than done.

The quickest way to get a multitude of things accomplished is to do just "one thing at a time."

If your method is "hit or miss" you will usually miss.

It is better to say, "This one thing I do," than to say, "These forty things I dabble in."

The church is full of willing people— some are willing to work, and the others are willing to let them.

For heaven's sake—what on earth are you doing?

Plan your work—then *work your plan.*

No work is so wearisome as doing nothing. (Arthur T. Pierson)

(See: Perseverance, Service, Zeal)

WORRY

Said the Robin to the Sparrow,
"I would really like to know
why these anxious human beings
rush around and worry so?"

Said the Sparrow to the Robin,
"Friend, I think that it must be
that they have no heavenly Father
such as cares for you and me."

Every tomorrow has two handles. We may take hold of it by the handle of anxiety, or we can take hold of it by the handle of faith.

The manicure business is falling off—too many people are biting their nails.

Those who joyfully leave everything in God's hand will eventually see God's hand in everything.

The reason worry kills more people than work is that more people worry than those who work.

Faith ends where worry begins, and worry ends where faith begins.

There is a great difference between *worry* and *concern*.

Worry frets about a problem
Concern solves the problem.

There are 773,692 words in the Bible, but not once can we find the word "worry" among them. The conclusion is obvious —if "worry" is not in God's vocabulary, it should not be in ours.

I joined the new "Don't Worry Club,"
   and now I hold my breath;
I'm so afraid I'll worry that
   I'm worried half to death!

Worry is an emotion that can never empty tomorrow of its problems, but it does empty today of its strength. It does not help us escape evil, but it does make us ill-prepared to cope with it when and if it comes.

Don't fret and worry about the future. Do what you know you ought to do today. The rest is God's responsibility. He has promised to be with us each step of the way. What more can we ask for?

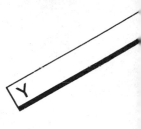

YIELDEDNESS

Defeat can be the begining of success . . .
a colt is not much good until he's been
broken. Neither are we.

You must be melted before you can be
molded.

"Lord, I want to throw myself blindfolded
into thy care." (George Whitfield)

(See: Commitment, Consecration,
Surrender)

ZEAL

Attempt great things *for* God.
Expect great things *from* God.
(William Carey)

It is better to have ignorance on fire than intellectualism on ice.

Let us not be *foolishly fervent* or *frigidly formal.*

Tear Out This Form
and Mail Today
SPECIAL PRICE

As you enjoy this treasury of quotes, you will probably think of others—friends and loved ones—whose lives would be blessed by this booklet.

If so, take a moment right now to order extra copies for gifts. The regular price is $2.95 each. Your special price from GRASON is 4 copies for $8.00 ($2.00 each) plus $.75 postage and handling. Any additional copies (more than 4) will cost you only $1.50 each.

☐ YES, please send me 4 copies of POCKET WISDOM at the special price of $8.00 plus $.75 postage and handling (regularly priced at $2.95 each).

___Additional copies for $1.50 each.

_____

Name

_____

Address

_____

City   State   Zip

Send this order form and your payment today to:

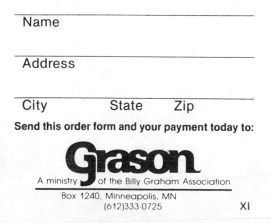

A ministry of the Billy Graham Association

Box 1240, Minneapolis, MN
(612)333-0725

XI